Nature's Juicehead

Presents

Prepped To Win

How to Contest Prep

For Amateurs

Nature's Juicehead©:

- Classic Physique Pro (Nspire Sports League)
- Lifetime Natural Bodybuilder
- NASM Certified Trainer (CES, PES, FNS)
- Instagram: @natures_juicehead
- College Graduate: F.I.U.
- Author: The Fat Cycling Method
  http://thefatcyclingmethod.com

COPYRIGHT

All Copyright ©2016–2017 by Carlos G. Hurtado, Nature's Juicehead©.

All Rights Reserved. No part of this book may be reproduced, replicated, and/or plagiarized in part or in full by any means, neither in electronic, paperback, or any other form.

It may not be stored in retrieval system, or transmitted, resold, in any form or by any means without prior written permission or consent of the publisher.

This title is only available from its official distributor. If you have purchased this book elsewhere, as an e-book, PDF, without a cover, or any other form whatsoever it may be illegally purchased. Please report this to the publisher.

DISCLAIMER

This book was written to explain the way I, Nature's Juicehead©, approach contest prepping. This is all based per my own personal experiences.

The advice given is not intended to cure or improve any injuries, illnesses, or diseases. Please consult with your doctor, nutritionist, and/or personal trainer before attempting any of the methods and techniques recommended in this book.

I am, by no means, a licensed nutritionist or doctor and as aforementioned, the results discussed are again, theoretical as per my own personal experience.

I am a Certified Fitness Nutrition Specialist and Certified Trainer through the National Academy of Sports Medicine (CES, PES, FNS).

CES = Corrective Exercise Specialist

PES = Performance Enhancement Specialist

FNS = Fitness Nutrition Specialist

My recommendations are intended to help amateur competitors learn about the proper way to prepare for a bodybuilding contest. They are also intended to educate amateur competitors about the problems with extreme programs.

Everything discussed is based on my own personal observations and experience. Many of the topics discussed are my opinion. You do not have to use or follow any of my strategies or methods.

Again, I strongly suggest and encourage you to consult with your doctor, licensed nutritionist and/or any specialist before you become involved in any activity that may pose any danger or hazard to your health.

Take all the necessary precautions when attempting any nutritional and fitness programs.

Should you not adhere to my recommendation to see a doctor, specialist, and/or nutritionist, you are voluntarily attempting all the nutrition, fitness, and recommended planning and hereby release Wealthy Carma, LLC, Carlos G. Hurtado (the author of this book) and any affiliates from any responsibility due to misuse, misinterpretation, or anything that poses a danger to yourself, including side effects, sickness, and possibly death.

ACKNOWLEGEMENTS

   I would like to thank my mother, my father, and my family for all their support. Without my parents I wouldn't be who I am today. They've sacrificed everything to give my siblings and I the life they never had.

   I'd like to thank my partners and ex-employers for giving me the opportunity to grow as a person and trainer.

   I would also like to thank my friends and teammates (including those who have passed on) for their advice, help, influence, and loyalty. You have all inspired me to improve and push further than I ever thought possible.

   I would like to give a special thanks to my sister, Genesis Hurtado, for working extremely hard in the creation of this book.

Last but not least I'd like to thank all my clients, my fans, and my followers for staying true and loyal. You have trusted me with my expertise and have made this career choice of mine the best decisions I ever made.

TABLE OF CONTENTS

Chapter 1: Setting Goals & Picking a Contest 9
HOW TO KNOW IF "YOU'RE NOT READY": 11
WHAT IFS: 11
Here's how today, gurus' address "carbing up": 12
THE PRICE OF RUSHING INTO A COMPETITION 14
CALCULATING WEEKS OUT: 15
Setting up a timeline: 16
Calculating fat calories: 16
Calculating daily caloric deficit: 16
Calculating weeks out: 16
Note for Women: 18

Chapter 2: How do you choose a coach/guru? 20

Chapter 3: Proportion, Symmetry, Posing, Presentation, Conditioning, and Endurance 22
PROPORTION VS. SYMMETRY 22
POSING: 22
PRESENTATION: 23
CONDITIONING: 24
ENDURANCE: 24
Night Show (Round 2) Tips: 25

Chapter 4: Diet and Nutrition Truths 26
ARE ILLEGAL PED's NECESSARY? 27

Chapter 5: Peak Week 30
WATER MANIPULATION: 30
Sodium Intake: 31
Diuretics 31

CARBING UP:	32
Chapter 6: Natural "NATTY" vs. Enhanced	***34***
WHAT DOES IT MEAN TO BE NATTY?	34
WHAT DOES IT MEAN TO BE ENHANCED?	34
Possible side effects of PED abuse:	35
MY THOUGHTS ON ENHANCED ATHLETES:	36
Chapter 7: Tanning	***38***
MOST IMPORTANT TANNING TIPS:	39
Chapter 8: Mentality	***41***
Chapter 9: Critiques	***42***
Chapter 10: Evaluation	***43***
Chapter 11: Reality	***44***
SOCIAL MEDIA	45
ABOUT THE AUTHOR	46
PERSONAL CONSULTATIONS	48

Chapter 1: Setting Goals & Picking a Contest

Knowing how many "weeks out" you are from a show is, in my opinion, the most important part of competing. The term "weeks out" refers to the approximate number of weeks left before you step on-stage. The term "days out" can also be used when there's less than 14 days remaining. On social media, the hashtags #2weeksout for example, means you will be stepping on stage in about 2 weeks. #14daysout can also be used.

Competing has many variables that need to be considered in order to be successful. Those include but are not limited to; proportions, symmetry, posing, presentation, conditioning, and endurance (See Chapter 3-Pg. 22). The most important piece of advice I could ever give you is to be honest with yourself. Rushing into a competition can be disastrous to your image, self-esteem, and overall health.

Do the things I recommend in this book and do not let anyone, especially a coach or a guru, "rush" you into getting on-stage. Rushing the process produces more negative consequences then positives outcomes. The last thing you want is, for what's supposed to be an inspirational transformation journey, to become a stressful and counterproductive nightmare. I discuss this in great detail on "The Price of Rushing into a Competition", Pg. 14.

If your bodyfat is high, lean muscle mass is low, and body is not proportionate to the criteria in your division, do not try to make it work in 12 weeks! This will only set you back further and cause you to become discouraged rather than excited about competing.

If your coach forces you to perform two hours of cardio a day in order to achieve your goal, then he/she is not doing you any favors. Either this coach is ignorant or only cares about making money off you.

At 4 weeks out you should be close to being stage ready. At this point, your main concerns should be posing and presentation. You want the judges to see you smile and radiating with confidence. Your presentation is a "make it or break it" aspect of competing.

I like to do a trial "peak week", 3-4 weeks out, so that I can eliminate as many mistakes as possible. Once I enter my real peak week, I should be aware of all the adjustments I need to make, in order to look my best on the day of the show.

You are investing a lot of time and money in posing suits, tanning, travel, lodging, supplements, food, coaching, PED's, etc... why would you risk NOT looking your best by having only one peak week? Find out what works for you before you polish up the final product!

Many of these self-proclaimed gurus give the exact same protocol to all their clients, regardless of current state, as if everyone will react the same. If all their clients were clones of each other, that'd be fine, but they're not. People react differently to different programs depending on what they have adapted to.

What if the client needs to build up their shoulders? What if the client needs to build overall mass? What if a client has overpowering features? What if the client is new to weight training? These are just a few basic factors in prepping for a show that need to be addressed. A good coach will take a good look at you and give you an informative diagnosis. You can't train everyone exactly the same and expect different results.

HOW TO KNOW IF "YOU'RE NOT READY":

- If 12 weeks out you're still working or need to work on physical proportions (v-taper, shoulder to waist ratio, calf to bicep, etc.), **you're not ready!**
- If 4 weeks out you aren't doing "peak day" test runs because you're still not conditioned enough, **you're not ready.**
- If 2 weeks out you aren't focusing on posing and presentation rather than conditioning and proportions, **you're not ready.**

Building a proportionate body is something you work on in the off-season. If a coach tells you to start extreme dieting 12 weeks out from a show and you don't have the slightest idea about what the criteria is for your division, then this coach is either clueless or does not have your best interest at heart!

That's like buying a used car, from a shady dealer, while not asking for the car facts, who tells you its "perfect" while selling it to you at retail, with dollar signs in his eyes. Don't be a sheep!

If 4 weeks out you're still going hard with and an extreme calorie deficit and performing hours of cardio, either you're not ready or your coach is again, clueless! Sometimes a competitor is ready 6 weeks out and a coach will keep them on the same extreme regiment for the remaining prep time. It's absolutely crazy and counterproductive.

WHAT IFS:

Here are a few "what ifs" that explain why performing a practice peak week is CRUCIAL:

- What if you don't hit your peak week right?
- What if you drink too much water?

- What if you don't drink enough?
- What if you retain too much water?
- What if your carbs don't kick in fast enough?
- What if you cramp up severely?

Carbing up correctly is one of the hardest things to get correct on peak week. Your body takes a few days to digest any carbs you consume so timing is everything. Yes you consume carbs such as dextrose, white rice, russet potatoes, etc... that have high glycemic indexes, but even then it's risky business. I prefer to have my muscles full one week in advance and focus only on dryness.

If you speak to anyone who has ever competed, most will tell you that they looked better a day or two after the competition. Why is that? What can you do about it?

Here's how today, gurus' address "carbing up":

They make their athletes go into an extreme depletion period, peak week, and wait 1 to 2 days before the show to start consuming carbs. They recommend prescription insulin while consuming high glycemic carbs and prescription diuretics, to fill you up and dry you out respectively.

If you're a smart logical person, think about it, are you going to put foreign substances into your body without you having any idea how they might affect you? Prescription insulin is prescribed to diabetics who have lost the ability to produce insulin.

Can this method work? Yes, if everything goes perfectly according to plan, which rarely does. The bigger questions are, are you willing to lose insulin sensitivity and become a diabetic? Are you willing to go into an insulin shock and possibly die?

The biggest problem with drugs is that everyone's organism reacts differently to them. Not only drugs, but supplements, foods, and any other substances you consume or inject into your body. Humans have different absorption rates, deficiencies, and other factors that may cause adverse side effects such as rashes, dizziness, fatigue, and nausea. Be very careful when it comes to the use of drugs.

This is why you should be doing test runs 3-4 weeks out. To see how much time your body needs to digest and fill up your muscles and to see how you react to supplements. Take the "what if" variable out of the equation. I highly recommend at least one test run just to see what you can do better on your actual peak week.

Two weeks out, you should be focused on posing and presentation, I can't stress this enough! You should be allowing your body to recover and make anticipated adjustments as deemed necessary. You should have peace of mind and feel confident that you will look your best.

With that said, I've witnessed competitors who look ready to step on stage 4-6 weeks out maintaining an extreme regiment all the way into peak week. Why would they do that? When show-time arrives, their body is so depleted that their presentation is horrible. They can't think, move properly, and some either cramp up or shut down completely.

Again, be logical and honest with yourself. Do your homework, keep track of your measurements, and make wise decisions that will help you be your best. You don't have to go all out in one show.

The point of being an amateur is to improve, gain experience, and progress into a PRO.

THE PRICE OF RUSHING INTO A COMPETITION

A real coach, one with legitimate certifications and competition experience, will be honest and tell you whether or not you're ready to compete in 10-12 weeks. Furthermore, a legitimate coach will be able to tell you how much work you need if you aren't ready.

Please understand the following: if you aren't ready to compete now, it does not mean you can't use the services of a legitimate coach or trainer. How can you expect to ever be ready if you have no idea in what direction to go?

A good coach will help you with your proportions by putting you on the right weight training program. They'll help you get leaner with the proper nutrition plan. Be patient during the process. If done correctly, it will be one of the most rewarding and beautiful journey's you will ever take part in.

If you rush your prep, the following are the possible consequences you will most likely suffer from:

1. Significant loss of lean muscle mass.
2. Complete shutdown of your metabolism.
3. Malnutrition and deterioration of your overall health.
4. High risk of serious injury to your muscles and joints (tendons and ligaments).
5. Huge weight rebound, gaining more fat than what you started with.

As if everything I just mentioned wasn't bad enough, most people who go through these grueling preps, will attempt to do it again. Why? Because they feel guilty or ashamed that they gave up, broke down, or sabotaged themselves the last weeks. In reality, the only one at fault is the coach.

Before the grueling prep, these individuals were probably 12 months out from being ready to BEGIN "prepping" for a show. After the grueling 12 week prep, which didn't work the first time, they will now be 16 months out. The second round will be harder, more damaging, and will push them even further back. They will be weaker, malnutritioned, possibly sick and injured, and their rebound will be even greater than the first time. Until you fix what's damaged, the results will get worse, the rebounds will be greater, and the damage may become irreparable.

CALCULATING WEEKS OUT:

There's this unspoken rule in the industry today that you need to prep for 12 weeks before stepping on stage. It doesn't matter how far off you may be, you have to do it in 12 weeks. I for one, completely disagree and consider it counterproductive. This type of approach is widely practiced by ignorant coaches/gurus who do not value their athletes or simply don't know any better.

Can you be ready in 12 weeks? Yes, it's possible, but you need to have a solid base in order for this approach to be effective. You can't be 30% bodyfat, completely new to weight lifting, and expect to be ready in 12 weeks.

This is why, in my opinion, there is no set amount of weeks that should be standard. I like to give myself 12-16 weeks because I like to perform test peak weeks before I get on stage. If it's my first show of the year, I'll give myself 16 weeks in order to test drive. If I've already competed a couple times, 8-10 weeks is more than sufficient as I've already worked out most of the kinks in my prep.

Setting up a timeline:

A good amount of bodyfat in pounds to lose per week is 1-2 pounds. In my opinion, 1 pound of fat is a more suitable number to prevent damage to your metabolism and prevent malnutrition. It's also more manageable to keep a good state of mind.

Calculating fat calories:

The first thing in calculating your "weeks out timeline" is knowing that one pound of fat has about 4,200 calories.

How do we know this?

One pound is equivalent to 16 ounces. One ounce is equal to 28.8 grams. One gram of fat carries 9 calories.

16 x 28.8 x 9 = 4, 147 calories. If we round up, that is around 4,200 calories.

Calculating daily caloric deficit:

If you divide 4,200 by 7 days, that is equal to 600 calories per day. This means that to lose one pound of fat per week you need to create a caloric deficit of 600 calories per day. A caloric deficit means that you need to burn an extra 600 calories per day then what you consume. In my book, http://thefatcyclingmethod.com, I discuss calorie calculations and deficit in great details.

Calculating weeks out:

I am a classic physique competitor. In my off season, I don't bulk, I stay relatively lean keeping my bodyfat around 8% bodyfat per, using the bodyfat caliper tests. Right now I weigh about 180 pounds.

I know that around 4% bodyfat I can be competitive or at least be within striking distance from great conditioning. If I can get lower than 4% that is great. To get to 4% or lower I do have to go extreme but only towards the last 2 or 3 weeks. By the time I'm ready to push the limits, I've already mastered my posing routine.

At 180 lbs and 8% bodyfat, I carry about 14.4 pounds of fat. This means that I have around 165.6 lbs of lean body mass. If I multiply 165.6 x 1.04 this comes out to around 172.2 lbs.

This means that in order for me to be at 4% bodyfat, I have to weigh 172.2 lbs if I'm able to preserve all my lean mass. I'd have to lose a total of 7.8 pounds.

If I lose one pound per week, I can do this in 8 weeks. If I want to do it in 4 weeks, I'd have to double my calorie deficit. Even though it's possible, it is much more of a toll on your body that can produce counterproductive consequences.

In my case, I can be stage ready in about 8 weeks. I'd give myself 10-12 weeks so that I can perform a test "peak week" and push a little harder if I feel I'm not lean enough. Especially if I've already committed to a show.

The more fat per week you need to lose, the longer you should give yourself before stepping on stage. My advice is to get a bodyfat test, find your lean body mass, and multiply that by the bodyfat you need to be at. If you do a caliper test, forget about male and female. A 4% reading, doing an 8 or 9 point method, should be ideal.

Take it easy, slowly drop the bodyfat, and give yourself time to practice posing and stage presence. Posing practice on its own can be overwhelming when you have other things going on, such as training and dieting.

Visit my website, http://trainercarlos.com/weeks-out-sample-sheet/, to print out a "WEEKS OUT SAMPLE SHEET" and http://trainercarlos.com/weeks-out-blank-sheet/, for a "WEEKS OUT BLANK SHEET".

Note for Women:

Women in general carry more fat than men. Using a caliper test, using 8 points as a guide, the bodyfat reading doesn't matter. Just note that it's only an estimate! You want to use the calipers only as a guide for future reference. The only important piece of information is the skinfold measurement in millimeters (mm). The skinfold bodyfat test for women is completely inaccurate using the formula I provide. If you apply the formula and you get a reading under 6%, this means that your skinfolds are very low and you look very lean.

What I need you to understand is that the skinfold doesn't consider the fat you store in your breasts and other body parts women tend to hold more fat in. But since you aren't doing a pinch on your breast or any of those other body parts, the reading will be the same as if you were a male. If you were to take a bodyfat test on a Dexa Scan (most accurate), BodPod or underwater test, those readings will be much more different. I've done an underwater test and the cost is around $50. Dexa and BodyPod are much pricier but very accurate. In the end, unless you truly want to know with exact certainty or for comparison purposes, only use them as a guide for future reference.

If you decide to use calipers, which for me are more than enough, the lower your caliper measurements are per test site, the lower your overall bodyfat is. I would aim to measure 5 millimeter (mm) or under on all skinfold measurements.

If you are a do it yourselfer, the areas to measure that I recommend are bicep, tricep, chest, mid-axillary, abdominal, supriliac, kidney, thigh, and calf. If you have someone to help you, measure your subscapular. Always measure on the right side.

The way I use this for future reference is that I take both, the skinfold measurements and a progress photo. I know that with those measurements that's how I look at that point in time. If I bulk or for whatever reason I gain considerable bodyfat, then I'd have to match those measurements again, on my next cut, in order to look like that progress photo.

Watch my video on how to perform a skinfold measurements on my website. Link to video here:

http://trainercarlos.com/perform-skinfold-measurements/

Chapter 2: How do you choose a coach/guru?

Please don't put your trust on a coach because they are some type of "PRO"! Do your homework! This is your body and your life that you're putting in their hands. There is a huge difference between a competitive PRO and a specific specialty professional.

You see, a professional bodybuilder or athlete is a "PRO" at their respective sport. They are professionals at competing. Most of the times, these athletic professionals have another professional training them.

Professional baseball players, football players, bodybuilders, all have specific trainers and coaches to help them be their best. They have nutritionists, therapist, certified personal trainers, and many other people who are certified or licensed in different specialties helping them be their best. Does this mean these pro athletes know anything about training? Nutrition? Therapy? Absolutely not.

If I go to a dentist, he'll tell me I have to brush my teeth several times a day. He recommends toothpastes and toothbrushes that protect my teeth the most. He goes over brushing techniques and the importance of flossing. He might recommend a bleaching product to make my teeth whiter. Does knowing this information now make me a dentist? Should I open my dentistry practice and office? NO! The same goes for a prep coach.

Make sure that the coach you consider has credible certifications and not some $20, online certification. Make sure they don't just throw you into a vegetable and protein diet. There are countless coaches out there who say they don't do cookie cutter diets, but if you look closely they all preach the exact same thing. Protein, vegetables, and hours of cardio.

A legitimate coach, with credible certifications, should be knowledgeable of different nutrition and training strategies. They should be able to explain in great detail what the strategies purposes are. Their expertise should not be limited to "carb cycling plus hours of cardio". If you want to learn about an alternative way to get lean and build muscle, check out my book at http://thefatcyclingmethod.com. At least you'll learn about a new way of doing things and see if it works for you.

A good coach should be able to create workouts and nutrition plans to meet your prep goals. Prep goals include proportions, conditioning, and endurance. A prep coach that makes you do the exact same things as his other clients, without any reasoning or purpose, is a waste of money.

Do your research, do your homework, and put real effort into putting together the right team for your prep needs. In bodybuilding you don't need a doctor or licensed nutritionist to get results, but a knowledgeable trainer with legitimate credentials from legitimate sources should be able to steer you in the right direction.

With that said, a good coach will have a trustworthy team of experts in other areas, such as posing. They'd have contacts for massage and physical therapists. One coach can't do it all. Do your due diligence and build a TEAM of experts that can help you in a variety of areas.

My recommendation at the very minimum is to have a good prep coach with a good solid background in weight training and nutrition. The next important coach is your "posing and presentation" coach. Optional specialties can be massage and physical therapists.

Chapter 3: Proportion, Symmetry, Posing, Presentation, Conditioning, and Endurance

PROPORTION VS. SYMMETRY

Proportion is different to symmetry. You can be symmetric and not be proportionate. Just to be clear, being proportionate is not only having the right shoulder to waist ratio. It's the way your biceps look compared to your calves. It's how your quads look in comparison to your arms, waist, calves, etc... Proportion is an overall representation of your body. If you have extremely big arms, your shoulders may look small. If you have huge quads your calves may look small. Proportions is about flow, balance, and eliminating distractions.

Symmetry is how even your body would look if it was divided in half through a vertical centerline, a mirror image you may say. You are comparing the details of the left to the right. Are both your arms and legs the same size and thickness? Are both pecs the same size and thickness? One half of your body has to look as close as possible to the other side. That is symmetry. Like I said at the beginning, it's possible for you to be symmetrical and not be proportionate.

POSING:

Posing is critical to your overall competition prep. You should do your best to practice every chance you get. When you're working out, you should be practicing your posing. After your workout, you should dedicate 10-20 minutes to your posing. The more you do it, the more natural it becomes and the more comfortable you'll feel on-stage. You should record yourself or have someone, a posing coach preferably, take a look at you and see what areas you need to improve upon.

Posing will reveal to the judges all your flaws and highlight your strengths, if you know how to express them correctly. The point of posing is to hide the flaws and show off your strengths.

Do not take posing for granted. I've seen athletes with great conditioning, symmetry, and proportions lose to an inferior athlete simply because they did not know how to pose. It's that big of a deal!

My suggestion is to hire a posing coach to show you the basics and give you a strong base to work from. I would spend at least 5 sessions (minimum 30 min. sessions) with a posing coach. Take what you learn from each session and work on those things as much as possible before your next session.

There are so many little details that you need to master that a few sessions are mandatory in order to catch them all. This is one thing that even top professionals cannot go about on their own.

PRESENTATION:

Presentation is similar to posing but it's more of an extra. Presentation is how you present your body. From your tan, to your competition suit, to skin condition, make-up if required, grooming, etc.

Presentation includes intangibles such as your confidence. How you strut through the stage tells a lot about your demeanor. Are you fluid, are you comfortable, are you smiling, are you confident?

When you walk on stage you should believe in your mind that you are the winner. You should be telling yourself, "there is no way anyone can beat me today. I have worked hard, I am prepared, and I am ready to own the stage".

Presentation is worked on when you practice posing. You should be smiling in between poses, recognizing what muscles you're hitting, and squeezing on every pose. You should be saying to yourself, "boom, check out my back, check out these legs" and so on.

CONDITIONING:

Conditioning refers to how lean, full, and dry you are able to get. In the bodybuilding world, the goal you are trying to reach is usually described as trying to get thin skin. Another term commonly used is onion skin. At the most extreme levels it's basically having see-through skin.

The more conditioned you are, the less bodyfat you carry. In women's bikini, the conditioning doesn't have to be as extreme. But as muscularity goes up, so does conditioning.

ENDURANCE:

Endurance refers to the ability to hold poses for long periods of time. When you are on-stage, if you are one of the top 5 in a show, you will be compared to your competitors. Comparisons are performed when athletes are brought to the center stage through a process referred to as "call-outs". The first call-out is typically that of the best 5 athletes. They are lined up, moved around, and asked to perform mandatory poses. Once the judges are satisfied, they ask the first call-out of athlete's to exit the stage and the remaining call-outs are lined up and compared.

Depending how close the competition is, several rounds of posing, flexing, and twisting will take place per call-out. This can happen both in the morning and the night show. This is why when you practice your posing, you should include holding the mandatory poses for 10-20 seconds at a time. It could mean the difference between 1st and 5th place.

Do not take endurance for granted. When you're backstage you are usually pumping up by doing certain exercises for a few minutes at a time. Then, when you get on stage, you perform your routine and stand on the side while the other competitors perform theirs. After everyone does their routine, the call-outs will begin.

While you are waiting for the other competitors to do their routine, you should be in a flexed front or side position and not relaxed. You should be smiling and looking confident.

While holding poses, if you get tired, you can switch between a front and side pose to keep you busy. You don't need to squeeze hard on the side but again, don't relax! A judge who was impressed with you could be staring at you on the side. Put all these activities together and the experience can be a grueling one. Work on your endurance!

Night Show (Round 2) Tips:

In most competitions, you have an intermission between two competitive rounds. The morning show is typically referred to as pre-judging (NPC) or round 1 (NSL). The night show (NPC) or The Championship Round (NSL), is where placings are revealed and awards are presented.

Do not let yourself go off track during the intermission. Go and eat some food, keep sipping on water, but do not have a huge meal and start drinking a ton of fluid. Most of the time, placings are decided in the morning round. If placings are close, they will be determined at the night show. Going crazy with food and liquid during the intermission can end up costing you a few places in your standings. Stay sharp!

Chapter 4: Diet and Nutrition Truths

Listen, when it comes to nutrition, there's a great possibility that you will react differently to different nutrition plans, foods, and supplements. While that is true, it's not because you are genetically different than anyone else. Do some individuals have "better" more "responsive" genetics? Yes, but the in the end, the genes are the same. It's a matter of adaptation and activation.

Like playing sports, in order for you to be a champion, you must be willing to train harder and smarter than your competitor. Smarter training means hitting your weakness hard and turning them into strengths. In nutrition, it means forcing your body to adapt and perform the actions you need, such as boosting metabolism, burning fat, and/or induce the building of muscle.

The human body is a machine that has evolved over hundreds of thousands of years. In the end, we all work the same. It all comes down to what you train your body to do. If you run long distances for hours a day, your body will become very efficient at storing energy in the form of fat. If you want to be the best, you must be willing to do whatever it takes to reach that next level.

This is why I would never encourage a bodybuilding of fitness athlete to jump on a treadmill or any kind of cardio equipment for hours and hours. The most I'd recommend is 20-30 minutes a day. The higher the intensity the better.

Those people you see on the pro stage doing hours of cardio are on a bunch of anabolics, and even then they are losing muscle as the weeks go by. They try to get as huge as possible in the offseason, only to once again reduce their muscle mass.

For them, it's not a big deal because they are on the extreme side of things. They are "mass monsters". For an amateur and natural athlete though, this is extremely counterproductive. The less muscle mass you have, the slower your metabolism. The more extreme your caloric deficit, the slower your metabolism. The slower your metabolism, the more fat you store and the higher the risk for malnutrition.

The most important question is... at what cost are these extreme's worth it? I'll tell you the costs: malnutrition, stress, injury, fat gains, sickness, and many more negative effects. If you are a PRO, and consistently winning big shows making a great living out of it, it's absolutely worth it! If you're just an ordinary Joe who dreams of getting on-stage, it's not worth it. If you are a trainer using competition preps to motivate clients, it's not worth it. If it's not your livelihood, the possible damage to your health and body isn't worth it.

In the end, what's the justification for extreme actions? Hard work, dedication, and perseverance. Doing whatever it takes! But doing whatever it takes does not mean go ahead do dumb irresponsible things!

Honestly, I agree that competing takes all those things aforementioned. I for one, salute everyone who goes through a prep and steps on stage, but imagine how much better of an experience they'd have if they prepared smarter with that same enthusiasm. The results would be better, permanent and above all, enjoyable.

ARE ILLEGAL PED's NECESSARY?

PED's (Performance Enhancement Drugs) are basically any drug that improves your athletic performance and/or appearance. Steroids (juice), Trenbolone (Tren), growth hormone, insulin, testosterone, diuretics, etc... all these drugs are PED's and illegal if not prescribed.

I'm not going to be a hypocrite and say that PED's are completely unnecessary and not useful. In an ideal world, if everyone had the same responsive genetics and experienced the same muscle growth from lifting and nutrition, drugs would not be necessary. It'd come down to who worked the hardest!

The problem is that all things are not equal! Everyone wants an edge and as many shortcuts as possible. In that case, PED's are more than useful!

In Open Class Bodybuilding, at the 212 division, and even in Classic Physique, PED's are a necessity. Even with great genetics, a natural bodybuilder will always be at a disadvantage. By me saying this, I'm not giving you the green light to go ahead and use illegal and non-prescribed PED's. Although PED's can provide great benefits if used correctly, the side effects can also be serious and life threatening. Liver damage, enlarge organs, hormonal imbalance, loss of hair, shortness of breath, heart attacks... these are just a few side effects I can recall off the top of my head.

An amateur competing for fun or as a hobby does not need to mess around with illegal PED's. To be honest, if you are a Men's Physique or women's Bikini competitor, I would advise you to stay away from illegal PED's. The longer you can train your body naturally, the better the results you will get, should you ever decide to go the PED route.

Do PED's give you an advantage? Yes, if you know what you're doing. I for one, stay away from foreign illegal substances! My current and long term health is much too valuable to be jeopardized, with something I don't need.

My advice to anyone contemplating using PED's is to train naturally as long as possible. Learn to lift the correct way to induce muscle growth. Get your nutrition on point and find out how your body reacts to foods and supplements. Attempt to become a high level athlete naturally before you even consider putting anything inside your body that may hurt or even kill you.

Be realistic with yourself about how far you can go in the industry. Do your research on PED's, consult with a physician, and don't inject or insert anything foreign into your body that you have no idea about. Do not take anyone's advice without consulting a professional first. Your life is at stake!

Chapter 5: Peak Week

For me, peak week is about just that, reaching your peak form on the day of the show. Unless you take specific drugs/substances such as insulin and diuretics, you have to learn to work with nature. Our body has tendencies to do specific things in order to survive. It wants to stay in what is known as homeostasis and keep neutrality.

If you are a natural athlete, you have to learn to manipulate your body's tendencies. Use those tendencies to manipulate specific goals. Let me share with you a few things that you may already know but are common in the industry when it comes to peak week.

WATER MANIPULATION:

I like to start increasing my water no later than 10 days before my "peak day", the day I am scheduled to step on stage. More often than not, I give myself at least 14 days before "peak day". Fourteen days out, I increase my water intake to about a gallon and half. Every other day I increase that by ¼ gallon until I'm drinking around 2 – 2.5 gallons daily. I've drank as much as up to 3 gallons a day and honestly, that is way too much water for me.

Included in my water intake is the water I drink with my pre and post workout, but not the water I consume during my workout. I also exclude coffee and the water I drink with my protein shakes.

During this period of high water intake, you will be going to bathroom frequently. If you have a job, find a way to consume most of your water when you're not at work. You may have trouble sleeping because you'll be waking up frequently in the middle of the night. I try to drink most of my water 3 hours before I go to bed. This allows me to release a lot of water before bed but you may wake up a few times.

The point of drinking a lot of water is to overload the body and force it to flush out as much of that extra water as possible. Four days before stepping on stage, I cut the water down 1 gallon. Three days out, I drink about 80 ounces. Two days out, I drink half a gallon. One day out, I drink 8 ounces with each meal and sip on water the day of the show.

This is what works for me and you'll have to test drive it to see what works best for you. It is not easy! If you tend to retain water you'll have to start either cutting sooner or do a little more cardio that last week in order to sweat out as much water as possible.

Sodium Intake:

One week before "peak week", 14 days out, I keep my sodium high. I love spiciness in my food so I add tabasco sauce to just about everything. You can salt your food moderately and it'll increase your sodium intake. During those first 7 days, I easily consume about 3000 mg of sodium per day. The last 7 days (peak week), I taper it down little by little until I'm only getting in about 800-1000 mg per day for the final 4 days. The final four days typically range from Tuesday all the way into the show. The day of the show, I consume normal amounts of sodium but still keep my water intake low.

Diuretics

Getting rid of water is a tricky process. Diuretics definitely help but in the end they can only do so much. Prescription diuretics are powerful and may cause you to lose water from the muscles making you look smaller and flat. Natural diuretics include asparagus, cranberries, dandelion, and hawthorns. I purchase a supplement that has many of these natural diuretics in pill form. Visit my website http://trainercarlos.com/what-supplements-does-trainercarlos-use-and-why/ for the link to the natural diuretic I use personally.

Other ways to maximize dryness is to use a sauna or take a hot yoga class. As I have said many times before in this book, do not do extreme. Push the envelope as long as you feel well. If you get sick, dizzy, cramp up or get nauseous, STOP! Bring it down a notch, drink a little more water and rest up. The last thing you want is to cramp up at the show or end up in the hospital due to severe dehydration.

CARBING UP:

Carbing up on peak week for me is different from the normal approach of starving, depleting, and carb up starting Thursday or Friday. Some coaches and gurus recommend starting to carb up Friday night and into Saturday morning. In my opinion, this is a very risky and inefficient method.

It's inefficient because unless you're using certain drugs, the absorption of nutrients may take a while (48-72 hours) before your body allows it to happen. Your body needs to digest the food, produce insulin, and drive it into the muscles. Even with drugs, it's still risky as you may miss the mark. It's a shot in the dark at best!

This is why you should be ready to step on stage, conditioning wise, at least 4-5 weeks out. I like to start eating carbs 2 weeks out, filling up my muscles, letting the nutrients digest, which helps me recover and allows me to work out hard well into Thursday, before the show. This strategy keeps me sane and I can still keep a slight deficit to continue to lean out some more. If you're not maximally conditioned two weeks out, you're simply not ready and take it as a learning experience. The only thing I worry about is my water manipulation and sodium intake so I can maximize fullness and dryness on peak week. Remember that high cortisol levels, caused by stress, cause you to retain water and lose lean mass.

My nutrition approach is based on my own method, THE FAT CYCLING METHOD©, that I created and which you can purchase at http://thefatcyclingmethod.com. If you read my book, you'll see why I set myself up to be in Phase 3 of the cycle the last two weeks. I also use other natural supplements to control my insulin and sugar levels. I go into great details in THE FAT CYCLING METHOD©.

I like to have my last leg workout the Friday before peak week. From there on, I focus on upper-body and full-body power workouts that don't directly stress my legs. I start including HIIT cardio the last two weeks to help my body get rid of as much water as possible all while drinking high amounts of water. My last workout, on Thursday, is an all-out HIIT and Abs workout with a sweat suit to drop as much water as possible. That in a nutshell, is how I approach peak week.

Chapter 6: Natural "NATTY" vs. Enhanced

WHAT DOES IT MEAN TO BE NATTY?

A natural "natty" athlete is one who has never consumed illegal or prescription drugs without a prescription. If you take Clenbuterol, without a prescription, you are not natty! I had a coach tell me that if I took "Clen", I'd still be considered natty because asthmatic people are prescribed this drug. This person also told me, after I took an underwater bodyfat test, and measured 3.2%, that I still had to lose about 30 pounds. At that point I knew this individual could no longer be my coach.

If you take any illegal drug (testosterone, steroid, etc.) without a prescription, you are not natty! If you take a prescription diuretic without a prescription, you are not natty! It's pretty simple.

WHAT DOES IT MEAN TO BE ENHANCED?

Being an enhanced athlete simply means that you aren't natty. The main reasoning for taking illegal or non-prescribed drugs is usually as a shortcut or to get an edge, otherwise you'd have no need for it. I can't explain it any other way. With that said, taking illegal and non-prescribed drugs does not guarantee you will get any significant results. It does not mean you will perform better, get bigger, or make any type of gains. If you have no clue as to what a proper nutrition and weight lifting program looks like, no amount of drugs will ever give you any results.

I am a lifetime natural athlete, and as such, I can't give you any advice as to what it's like to take PED's. All I can do is share with you what I do know about PED's from my existence in the industry. Anabolics such as steroids aka "Juice",

Trenbolon aka "Tren", and Testosterone "Test" help athletes get stronger, increase muscle mass faster, and break muscular plateaus not possible naturally.

They help with the recovery of muscles after training and speed up the recovery of injuries. Other PED's such as Clen allow you to lean out faster to a level very difficult to obtain naturally. PED's, if abused or not used correctly, can be hazardous and even deadly.

In the body, we have vital organs and muscles that also experience growth in the presence of PED's such as growth hormones. PED's also throw your hormone production out of wack and for the most part, it's a once you go in, you don't come back kinda deal.

If you're willing to risk your quality of life with these substances, that is your prerogative, but if you cherish your quality of life, you'd stay away from them. On the same token, if you do go in that direction, please hire someone who knows what they are doing. If you have to pay more for their services, pay more! The saying "you get what you pay for" holds true in this area, both in consumption and the quality of the substances you use.

Just like hiring a trainer and/or coach, checking their certificates and reputation is extremely important. Deal with professionals, reputable doctors and nutritionist. Your life is at stake. Your future well-being is at stake. You risk everything by taking foreign illegal substances!

Possible side effects of PED abuse:

- Rashes and excess acne
- Baldness
- Diabetes
- Shortness of breath

- Extreme dehydration
- Palumboism
- Serious injuries (muscle tears, joint damage...etc.)
- Sexual performance
- Death

The aforementioned are only some of the possible side effects. Please know that once you get off PED's, you will lose any gains you may have experienced.

As a natural athlete, I use science to my advantage. I change my workout routines depending on what diet or phase I am in. Slowly but surely I been able to add a lot of muscle to my frame and have a respectable body that technically, is not achievable by natural standards. I say this according to the FFMI "Free Fat Mass Index" calculator.

We are in a different era. We have so much knowledge at our hands that not getting result is a matter of ignorance, laziness, and lack of determination.

Can I be much bigger and stronger with the aid of drugs? Absolutely! But I cherish my life, my body, and do not want to die of a heart attack before I even turn 50. I don't want to be crippled with joint problems, sickness, and a host of other problems once I retire and get off all the drugs.

MY THOUGHTS ON ENHANCED ATHLETES:

Honestly, I could care less about whether someone takes PED's or not. I compete because I have a passion for fitness and competition. I, personally, have no interest in becoming a mass monster! I want to have a lean muscular aesthetic body.

I am willing to work hard for my results and I'm intelligent enough to maximize results without drugs. I am also patient and vow to lead my clients, followers, and fans by example. Anyone who knows me and has seen the effort I put in the gym cannot deny that I give my everything every single day.

My work doesn't end in the gym, I also play around with different nutrition strategies, natural supplements, workout strategies, and perform hours of research weekly to maximize performance. I am a student of the game always expanding my horizons.

Even though I am bigger and leaner than the average gym goer, my results have been the product of all my hard work and extensive research. I'm not going to brag or claim that I know more than anyone in the industry, but if you want to learn everything I know, invest in my books and follow me on social media. I am determined and willing to share my knowledge with as many people as I can.

The Fat Cycling Method contains everything I've learned and researched about nutrition to this day. Prepped to win contains all my competition experience and a whole lot more.

In conclusion, the most important thing about drugs that you need to understand is that, unless you are deficient, your body is being forced to produce additional and excess hormones. This may cause a hormonal imbalance from which your body will do whatever it has to do to balance that out. If you produce extra testosterone, it will shut down your natural production and produce estrogen. If your body finds excessive growth hormones in your body, it'll shut down its production at the pituitary gland. Be careful, do your homework, find a trustworthy source, and do not put anything into your body that you are not comfortable with.

Chapter 7: Tanning

One of the most important aspects of bodybuilding is the quality of your tan. Looking dark isn't the only purpose of a tan. A great tan shows your definition, enhances your lines, and gives you that all-star look on stage. The judges will be able to better appreciate all the details that you've worked so hard for.

Tans are not cheap. Although you can purchase a "do it yourself" kit or "apply it yourself" tanning lotions and creams, the quality of the tan you can get at the show are hard to beat.

If you're serious about competing and looking your best, my suggestion is that you get a tan with the sponsoring tanning company at the show. If you're an amateur and just testing the waters, you can definitely try a "do it yourself" product such as Dream Tan, which is excellent, but if not applied correctly, could end up costing you several placings. There are so many variables that go into tanning that it may take a few practice applications before you get it right.

Most shows have check-ins the day before. The tanning companies are available at these check-ins and it's when you'd get your first and second coat (if necessary). Try to make an appointment in advance because if you wait until check-ins, you may not be able to get a tan or you'll have to wait for hours before a spot opens up. If you need two or more coats, you'd come the next day to get your additional coats as necessary. Many times they will spray a little shine on you, whether you used their services or not, right before you step on-stage. Just ask.

Again, you can do it yourself, but using an on-site tanning company would be my recommendation. Most of these on-site or sponsor tanning companies charge between $130-

150 for two coats. If you are pale, and need extra coats, the cost may be higher, but don't be afraid to ask for a discount.

My advice to you is to make sure they do a superb job with your tanning. You need to ensure that they cover all the angles and tricky spots such as; under the arms, obliques, and below the armpits. Don't be afraid to ask for a re-do in areas you see weren't covered correctly even after you have left your initial appointment. You can also get touch-ups on the day of the show as necessary at no additional cost. You paid for it, get it right!

You have spent months dieting, exercising, and posing your butt off. It'd be a shame to let such a small thing such as a missed spot or a poorly applied tan to cost you a placing or multiple placings! A great tan is a CRITICAL part of your presentation!

MOST IMPORTANT TANNING TIPS:

- Contact the tanning company a week in advance to get recommendations on how to get the best tanning experience. Some recommend certain products to exfoliate and clean the skin. These products are optional. I have clean hairless skin that soaks up the tan very well so I do not need these additional steps. But you might!
- Wear black loose clothing to check-ins before getting your tan. Do not wear red! Red clothing can turn your tan green.
- Wear underwear that you don't care about staining. I like to wear black boxers and raise them up my thigh as high as possible. If you aren't shy, you can even tan nude.

- Do not take your black loose clothing off for any reason. Liquid spills can happen and destroy your tan. Be especially careful if you have to go take a leak. Be safe about it.
- Take extra covers if you are staying at a hotel to avoid staining the hotel sheets.
- Make sure your hair is ready to go if you don't have a hairdresser or someone there to help you. Be groomed before getting your tan. Wetting your hands or gelling up can be disastrous!
- I would ask to have my face tanned. It can look strange to have your body tanned and your face pale. It's a big contrast!
- Shave everything, including armpits and bikini areas.
- Last but not least, have fun and don't panic. Focus on what you'll be doing on stage. If you do everything I mention here you won't have any problems.

Chapter 8: Mentality

When I compete, I compete to win! I have prepped way too long and way too hard to even think about anything, but first place. Yes you want to be a sportsman. Yes you want to be respectful. In the end, your frame of mind should be to dominate. If you don't show confidence you will come off as shy and timid. Get pumped up, get excited, and shine on stage!

Competing is a selfish sport. When you train, you're training YOUR body. When you meal prep and follow a specific nutrition plan, you are doing it for YOU! When you practice your posing you are practicing for YOU. Everything that you do you are doing it to ensure that judges have their best look at YOU! The whole contest prep is for YOU!

Competing is not for everyone. You must be willing to put the hours, the weeks, the months, and do everything necessary to be your best. You must be willing to give up weekends with friends to avoid drinking and falling off-course with your nutrition.

The sport on its own is a lifestyle, a way of living, and is a beautiful thing! In the off-season you work on your flaws but you are free to enjoy life again. Going through a prep though will change your outlook in life. Your life will change drastically. You will be stronger and more confident then you have ever been. You will make better decisions and recognize what's best for your health. You will avoid toxic situations. That is the point! To improve as a person, mentally and spiritually.

You are now prepped to win! Be confident, take pride in your work, smile, be sassy, and be strong.

Chapter 9: Critiques

Getting feedback from judges is critical to your progress. In an ideal world, judges should be able to give you immediate feedback after a show without a problem. The truth is that seldom does this happen.

Some contests and categories have a very large number of competitors. It is practically impossible to remember every single weakness, lacking body part, and other details of every single competitor.

The NSPIRE Sports League (NSL) uses the latest advances to allow judges to give feedback in real-time. Regardless of the technology being used, it is always a great idea to introduce yourself, give the judge your name and competition badge number in a little paper, or business card. By doing this, you increase the odds that they'll recognize you on-stage and give you a better evaluation and critique.

If you don't compete at the NSL, let me tell you how to go about getting a critique. Before the show begins, find and introduce yourself to the head judge and the other judges if possible. Engage in a little conversation, give them your badge number in a little piece of paper, and ask them to provide you with a critique. When the show is over, find them and ask them for your critique.

Communication with a judge is key to having a successful showing at your contest. They're the only ones who can tell you what they are looking for and how you can improve. On top of that, if they like you, they will remember you on your next showing.

Chapter 10: Evaluation

Once you get your critique you will know what areas you need to improve on. The three main areas you need to focus on is body proportions, conditioning, posing, and routine.

Make sure that you do your homework and find out what measurements your body needs to be at, depending on your category, in order to be competitive. Research the proportions from the top athletes in your category and try to achieve those same proportions. By proportions I mean hip to waist ratio, shoulder to hip ratio, etc.

Your conditioning is critical to a show. Conditioning refers to how lean, dry, full, and hard you look on stage. If you aren't lean, neither your lines nor your definition will clear. If you aren't dry, it'll look as if you weren't lean. You'll look "soft and bloated". Looking full has to do with the glycogen stores in your muscle. Usually, this is achieved by carbing up and filling up your glycogen stores.

In the typical bodybuilding arena, this achieved by a carb depletion on peak week followed by the high consumptions of carbs starting 2-3 days before stage day. I on the other hand have a different approach to dieting and prep as discussed earlier.

If you want to learn my nutrition and weight lifting secrets, check out my book "The Fat Cycling Method$^©$".

Order at http://www.thefatcyclingmethod.com

Chapter 11: Reality

The reality is that most athletes don't become professionals. Even if you have the honor of becoming a professional bodybuilder or athlete, it does not mean you will be rich and famous. When you leave the amateur ranks you enter a much higher level of competition than you ever thought possible.

The best mentality is to compete as a way to keep yourself in check. If you're a personal trainer, use it to keep yourself in shape year round and your clients motivated. It's a great conversation starter and it speaks volume about your character as a person.

Even though you may not become rich via the professional circuit, being a competitive athlete can give you credibility with potential clients. You may even become a sponsored athlete and at the very least have your supplements paid for.

As an athlete, do not fall for the guru trap. It's okay to get help, join a team, and hire a coach. All that I ask is to make sure that you aren't dealing with clueless individuals.

Whether we like it or not, politics play a big role in competing. It shouldn't, but it does. Just make sure that if you join an important team or hire a coach who is an influential figure in the sport, you have the freedom to not do things that can potentially hurt you.

Just because an athlete is nationally qualified or a PRO, it does not mean they have the slightest clue about strategizing, nutrition, and/or weight training principles.

Want me to work with you directly? Email me with subject: Contest Prep at workwithme@trainercarlos.com

SOCIAL MEDIA

Instagram: @natures_juicehead

Website: http://trainercarlos.com

FB: https://www.facebook.com/trainercarlosfitness/

HASHTAGS: #competetowin #naturesjuicehead

ABOUT THE AUTHOR

Carlos G. Hurtado, aka, Nature's Juicehead© is a Certified Personal Trainer and Professional Bodybuilder.

Nature's Juicehead© grew up playing sports, mainly baseball, most of his life up until college.

He graduated from College with a Degree in Civil Engineering and worked as a General Contractor for 5 years.

He became overweight and decided to go back to his fitness roots and pursue a career as an athlete and personal trainer.

Nature's Juicehead© received his certifications from the National Academy of Sports Medicine (NASM) and was trained by some of the most knowledgeable trainers in the world.

Since making the career switch, he has dedicated most of his time to learning from the top trainers, educators, and experts in the world.

With an engineering mind, where facts and research matter, he absorbed, researched, and tested everything he ever learned.

This has instilled a level of knowledge so deep that results are virtually guaranteed by his side.

As a competitive bodybuilder, Nature's Juicehead© discovered a method to shred fat, build muscle, and stay lean year round without the use of any illegal drugs. This method is THE FAT CYCLING METHOD©.

It is an accomplishment that he shares with you in this book and knows that those who apply his method correctly and responsibly, will achieve significant results.

Follow Nature's Juicehead© on Instagram (natures_juicehead_nslpro) and Facebook to witness first-hand how he uses his system to stay in the best shape of his life.

You will also have the opportunity to take part in live Frequently Asked Question Sessions he hosts live on Facebook as well as informative YouTube videos.

PERSONAL CONSULTATIONS

Everything you will ever need is in this book. Please use it wisely and responsibly.

Once you have read the book, make sure you take all your measurements, do all your calculations, and choose your meal plans as recommended. Make all the necessary modifications and adjustments to your nutrition plans and workouts as you see fit to achieve maximum results.

Post your customized nutrition plan on the refrigerator or use an app such as myfitnesspal to track your calories, macros, and fitness activities. Good luck.

Want me to guide you personally?

Email me at training@thefatcyclingmethod.com for private one-on-one consultation services and quotes.

Made in the USA
Middletown, DE
09 December 2018